this journal belongs to:

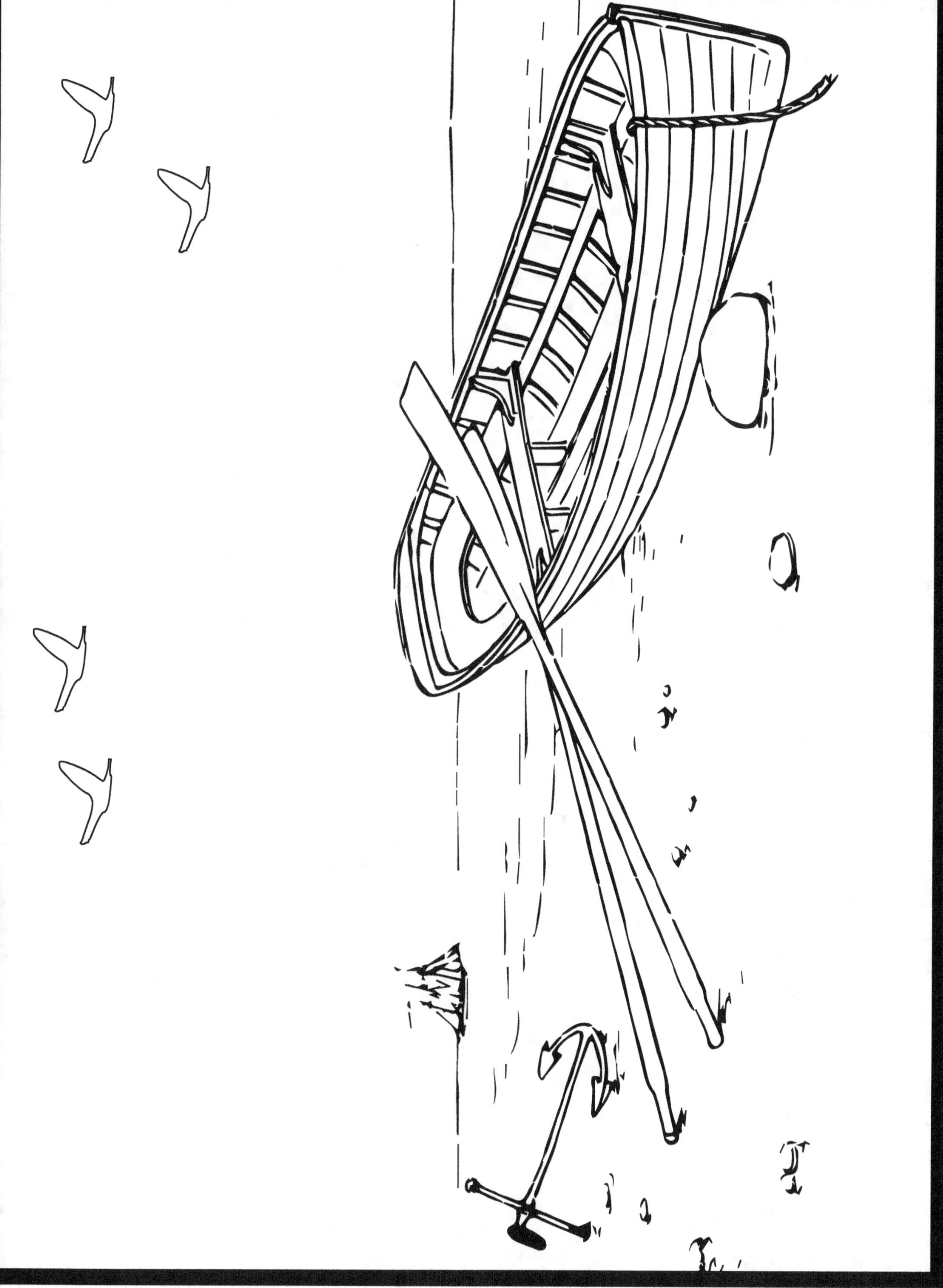

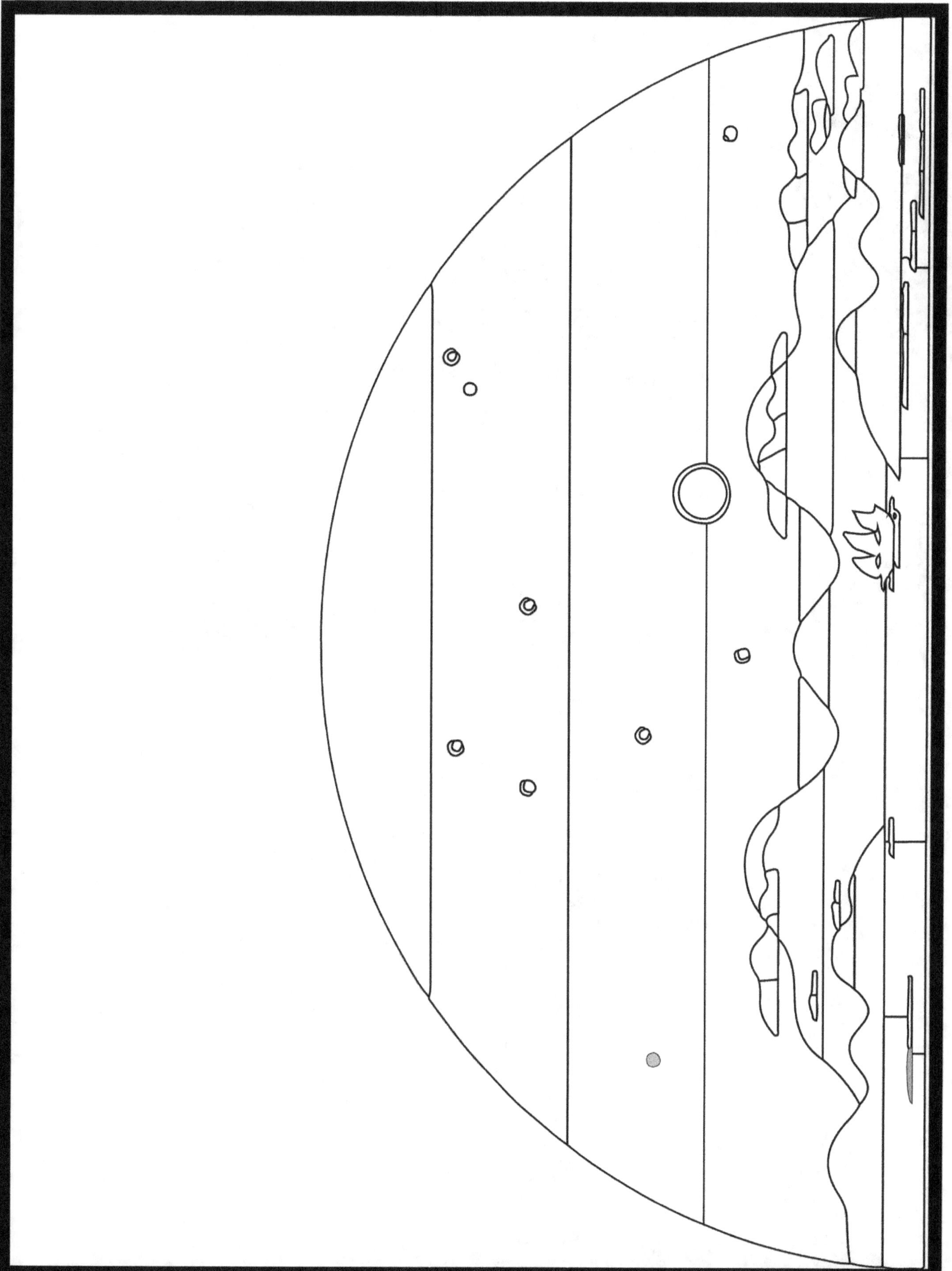

بـ

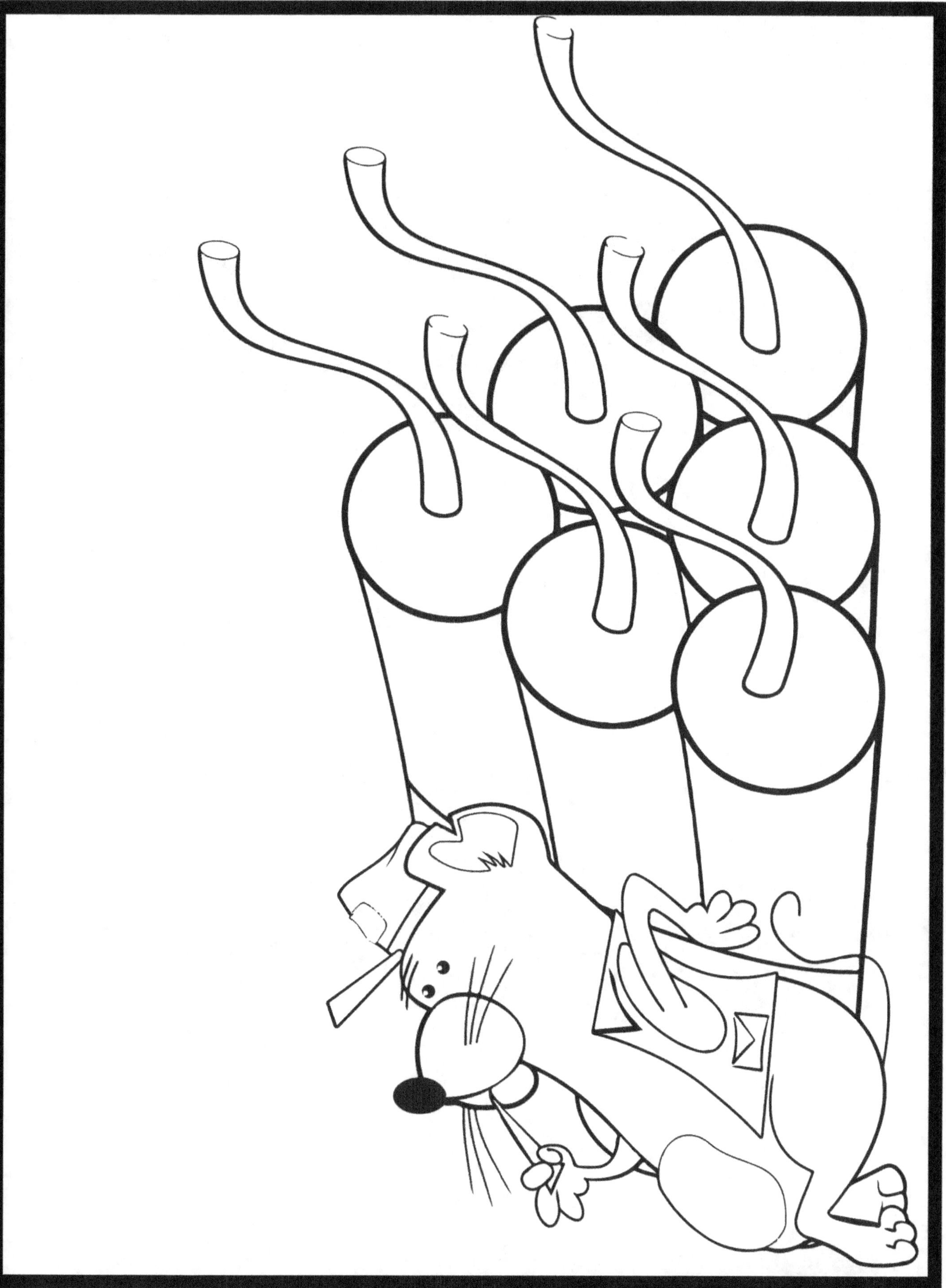

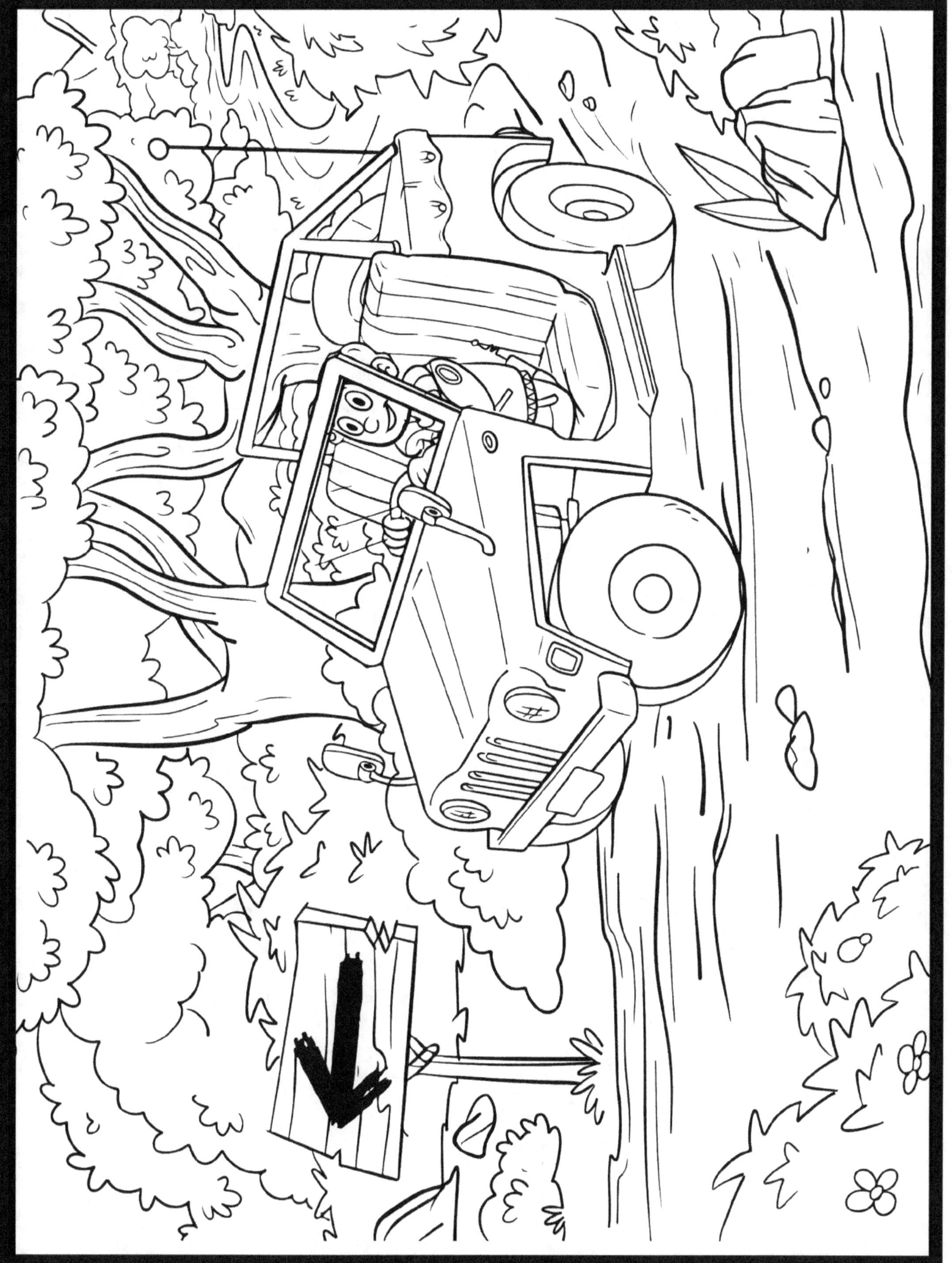

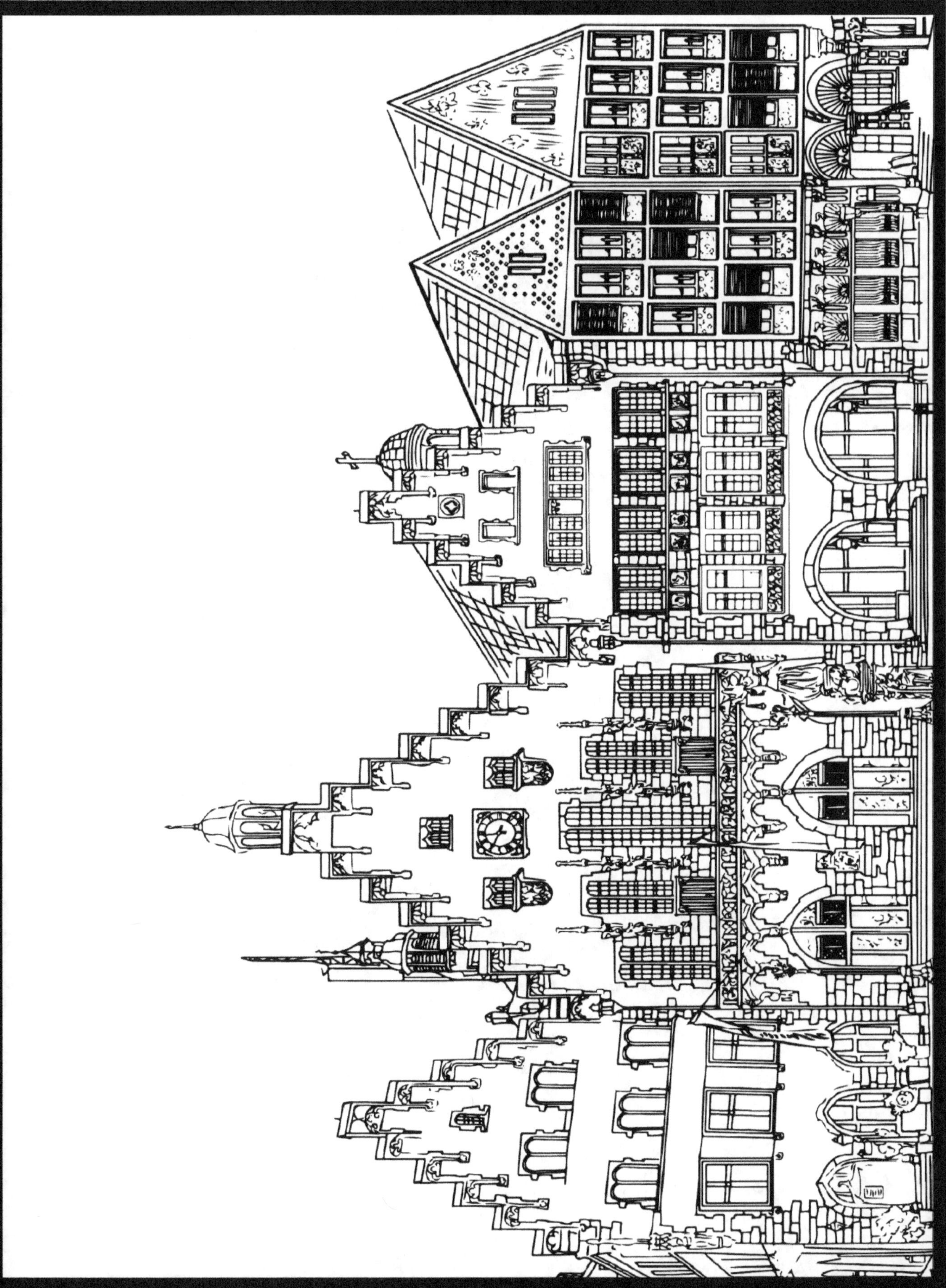

9 781677 334957